LIVING

IN THE

REALM

OF THE

SPIRIT

LIVING
IN THE
REALM
OF THE
SPIRIT

by

Frederick K.C. Price, D.D.

FAITH ONE
PUBLISHING

LOS ANGELES, CALIFORNIA

Unless otherwise indicated, all Scripture quotations are taken from the *King James Version* of the Bible.

3rd Printing

Living in the Realm of the Spirit
ISBN 1-883798-07-08
Copyright © 1989 by Frederick K.C. Price, D.D.
(Revised Edition 1995)
P.O. Box 90000
Los Angeles, CA 90009

Published by Faith One Publishing
7901 South Vermont Avenue
Los Angeles, California 90044

Contents

1
The Power of the Spirit

About thirty-five years ago, I was born again and called to preach the Gospel, and for the next seventeen years I really struggled in the Christian life. I had my ups and downs, but it was mostly downs. When I would read the book of Acts it would stick in my craw; it bothered me. I was not seeing the manifestation of the signs and wonders of Acts in my ministry, and I knew of very few other ministries where there were supernatural manifestations.

I began to cry out to God. I knew that He had called me, but I was ready to give up the ministry, because there was no power in me. I was dissatisfied. My own life was a wreck — an absolute shambles — when someone gave me a copy of Kathryn Kuhlman's book, *I Believe in Miracles*.[1] Then I knew that the signs and wonders were a reality; I knew that what the Bible said was alive today. So in 1970, I was filled with the Holy Spirit.

Shortly thereafter, someone gave me some books by a man named Kenneth Hagin that forever transformed my life. I read *What Faith Is, Right and Wrong Thinking, The Authority of the Believer*[2] and several other books. I had received the power in the Spirit of God, but I did not know how to harness that power to my life.

---

[1]Published by Prentice-Hall, Inc., Englewood Cliffs, New Jersey, 1962.
[2]Published by Kenneth Hagin Ministries, Tulsa, Oklahoma.

Over the years, I have seen many who were truly filled with the Spirit and had the power of God in their lives, but that power was not really transforming and changing their lives.

You can compare it to an automobile. You can have one of the most powerful engines in the world, capable of speeding a car down the road at two hundred miles per hour. But if you do not have a gear box and drive train to transfer the power of that engine to the wheels of the car, it will not go anywhere.

So you can have the power, be full of the Spirit of God, and speak with tongues, yet still abuse your spouse and family. You can be bound by everything you can think of until you learn how to harness that power to the wheels of your life.

Two-fold Purpose

I believe in the signs and wonders, and they are manifested in my ministry as the Spirit of God directs and as He wills. But whether you realize it or not, signs and wonders are not primarily for Christians. God has a two-fold purpose for the gifts of the Spirit:

First, they are to empower the ministry gifts — the apostles, prophets, evangelists, pastors, and teachers. They will operate in any Spirit-filled believer as the Holy Spirit wills, but mostly they are the tools of the trade for the ministry.

Second, they are God's method of advertising — not for Christians, but for sinners. The signs and wonders are so the world will know the reality and the power of Almighty God.

The Bible does not say that without the gifts of the Spirit it is impossible to please God. It says **without faith it is impossible to please him** (Heb. 11:6). God does not require sinners to exercise faith; it is impossible for them to do so. They are spiritually dead, and there is no way they can have the faith of God. But God expects His children to operate by faith.

We are not supposed to walk day by day by the gifts of the Spirit. We are supposed to walk day by day by faith. Do not think that sunrise to sunset is going to be one miracle after another, one supernatural manifestation after another, because it is not.

I expect the gifts of the Spirit to operate in my ministry, and they do. But for me, personally, to walk with God, I have to walk by faith. And so do you.

The Supernatural Realm

Signs and wonders are one side of the coin. Faith is the other side. Both of them move you into the realm of the spirit. Both of them are direct involvements of the supernatural realm in the natural realm.

There is a place in God where we can rise above the circumstances of the natural, but very few people seem to understand it. Here is an example from my own life:

I found out about divine healing about the same time I found out that the book of Acts was alive today, that it would work today. I learned that it was God's will for me to be well. I discovered that I could

9

walk in divine healing. This was great, because I had always been sick with something.

Man, I waited for Satan to put some kind of sickness or disease on me, so I could take my new-found power and knock it in the head in the name of Jesus. I was walking around, waiting for the enemy to attack me with something, so I could pull out my sword of divine healing and whack away at it. I was ready. I was armed with divine healing. Everywhere I went I was looking for sickness to attack me, and of course it did.

Then one day I heard a man say he had never had a headache in thirty-seven years. I said, "What? Did he say he had never had a headache in thirty-seven years?" I began to listen, and suddenly the Spirit of God gave me a revelation. I found out that God's best is not divine healing — divine health is God's best. With divine health, you do not need to be healed.

Now thank God for divine healing. I am not knocking it, because divine healing can bring you to divine health. But so many in the Charismatic renewal are still waiting for all the problems and all the attacks of the enemy to come, so they can stand against them.

Above the Circumstances

Why should we walk in that garbage all the time? Why should we struggle under that kind of load? *We can rise up and live above the circumstances of our everyday lives.* There is a place where we can walk in God above the circumstances.

Of course, you have to choose to do it. But you cannot do it if you have a pity-party attitude. A lot of folks still want to cry. They enjoy crying and do not want to admit that they are on an ego trip. It makes them feel good to stand up and say, "Oh, I've had all these trials and all these tribulations. I don't know what I'm going to do. It's been so rough. Give me a little pity. Somebody feel sorry for me. I'm really having a hard time."

Well, I refuse to dishonor my Lord that way! Jesus is my example. Hebrews 12:2 says, **Looking unto Jesus the author and finisher of our faith.** Do not look at the circumstances. Do not look at the devil or his demons. Look to Jesus. He is the pattern, the schematic diagram, the blueprint, the example. He is the leader, and no matter what may come, I will follow Him. If I have to follow Him by myself, then so be it. I am going for God's best, and I do not believe in settling for less than the best.

God gave His best for us, and I believe God wants us to walk in His best. If He did not want us to, then why did He provide it? Why did He tell us about it?

If you want to please God and walk in His best, you have to make the choice to walk by faith.

2
Faith Is Now

Now faith is the substance of things hoped for, the evidence of things not seen.

Hebrews 11:1

Some years ago when the Lord gave me my assignment, I began to teach that faith has a time. In other words, there is a time when faith is faith, and there is a time when faith is not faith. So I taught that the word *now* in Hebrews 11:1 meant a time.

Then one day, I was teaching in a certain place, and a lady wrote me a very nice letter full of fire. In essence, she told me I was off in my teaching, because I did not realize that the word *now* is not in the original Greek text.

Well, I am a person who changes. I do not have a problem with changing if I find out I have been wrong. I will change instantaneously. It does not matter what anybody thinks about it. I intend to be right.

So I began to search it out to find out if she was right or if I was right. If I was wrong, I was going to change.

Sure enough, she was right. *Now* is not in the Greek text. It is not a time indicator in that verse. It really functions as a conjunction to connect the last verse of chapter 10 to the first verse of chapter 11. A better translation could be "therefore" or "but." It could read like this: **But we are not of them that draw back unto perdition; but of them who believe to the saving of the soul.** (*Therefore*) **faith is the substance of things hoped for** (Heb. 10:39; 11:1).

So I had to figure out what was going on. I knew that time was involved with faith. And I knew that this was where most people were missing it with faith. If you do not understand that there is a time to faith, you cannot really walk in faith. You can spell it, and you can say it, but you will not walk in it until you find out about the time of faith.

I took another look at Hebrews 11:1 and said, "All right, if I drop the word *now*, capitalize the 'F' and make *faith* the first word of the sentence, then it would read like this, 'Faith is ....' Wait a minute. 'Faith is?'"

Then I saw it! The word *is* is a present tense verb. It could say 'Faith was,' and it could say 'Faith will be,' but, no, it says 'Faith is.' When it says 'Faith is,' it means right now — present tense. So I was back in the game, and I said, "Okay, I will teach it this way. I can still prove it by the Word of God. Faith *is*."

I kept meditating on the verse and said, "Well, let me add a little something here. Let me play with the English a little. I could say it like this, 'Faith is now.' Or I could say 'Faith is.' Or I could say 'Now faith is.' I am back to square one. Faith is present tense. If it is not present tense, it is not faith!"

Not in Agreement

Whenever you say, "I know God is going to do something," you are not in faith. You are not operating in faith, and that is why things are not working. Most people do not realize it, but when they say God is going to do something, they are saying He has not done it. He said He did it; you said He did not. God cannot get in agreement with you, because you are not in agreement with Him.

First Peter 2:24 says, **by whose stripes ye** *were* **healed.** It does not say you *will be* healed. It says you *were* healed. If you *were* healed, then you *are* healed right now; it is already done. You cannot receive the healing for yourself on your own faith until you realize that you have to receive it in the now. You cannot say that you know the Lord is going to heal you. You can die making that confession, because that is future tense, and faith is present tense.

Going on with Hebrews 11:1, it says, **Now faith is the substance of things hoped for.** That means that hope does not have any substance for what I am hoping and praying. Hope will not do you any good until you join faith with it. Hope sets the goal. If all you have is hope, then all it will allow you to do is smile while the ship is sinking. But if you put faith with the hope, you will keep the ship afloat. That is a big difference!

Faith is the substance, but what is substance? Substance is something that you can contact with your physical senses. It is something that can be seen, smelled, heard, tasted or touched. It is tangible. Hope does not have any substance.

If you are hoping God is going to heal you, you had better get a good doctor, because Satan is trying to give you a one-way ticket to the graveyard. Sure, you are sincere, but so was the gangster who broke into your house and ripped off your television set. He was sincere, too, but he was sincerely wrong.

So **faith is the substance of things hoped for, the evidence of things not seen.** Faith is the evidence, but what is evidence? Evidence is proof, and proof substantiates or validates the existence of something you do not presently have. If you already had it, you would not need any proof of it, because you have it. Proof takes the place of what it is the proof of until the thing arrives, therefore, proof is temporary.

Faith for each situation of life is temporary until that situation manifests itself. When the situation manifests, then you do not need any more faith for it, because you have it in manifestation.

If faith is the evidence or proof, then faith itself must be something. If it were not something, it could not be the proof.

Outside the Senses

Now notice this: it says faith is **the evidence of things not seen.** When we walk by faith, we leave the realm of the senses, and that is where most of us mess it up. We walk by the senses and not by faith. We walk by the circumstances. We magnify the circumstances. We rejoice in the circumstances. We even make jokes about the circumstances.

How often have you heard someone say, "I'll tell you what, I have the devil on the run, bless God. But the devil sure was chasing me." That is the mentality. They get up in church and brag about how hard they are having it. That gets them a little sympathy from people, but it does not honor God. There is no faith in it. I used to talk about the problem, thinking that I was being honest. But then I wised up and brought my words into line with God's Word.

I believe that when the Bible says that faith is **the evidence of things not seen,** the word *seen* does not mean just visual perception. That would leave out all you can hear, all you can smell, all you can taste and all you can touch. A better way to say it is that faith is the evidence of things not perceived by the senses.

Now if faith is the evidence of things not perceived by the physical senses, then that means there is another realm. There has to be another world, another realm where faith is the law.

We live in this three-dimensional world where our senses are the law. It is hot because we feel like it is hot. It is blue because we see that it is blue. It is sweet because we taste the sweetness. It is a discord because we hear that it is discordant.

Our senses are the law of the physical world, but when we walk by faith, we leave the physical world and enter the world of the spirit — God's world. In the spirit world, faith is the law, and if we do not operate in faith, we are going to be arrested for operating outside the law.

Faith is the law of the spirit realm, and faith is the key that allows us to enter that realm.

3
Faith and the Word

In chapter two, we established that faith is the substance or proof of things not seen or perceived by the senses. If that is the case, then how will I ever know at any one given point in my life what my faith is the evidence of if I have never seen or perceived what things are in the spirit realm?

If I have never been informed about what things are in the spirit world, how will I know? In other words, if I had never seen an elephant, how would I ever know that at any given point and time that my faith is now the evidence of an elephant?

There has to be something that tells me there is something out there in the spirit realm at any given time of which my faith is the evidence. I cannot have faith for it if I do not know that it is there.

Look at Romans 10:8:

> **But what saith it? The word is nigh thee, even in thy mouth, and in thy heart: that is, the word of faith, which we preach.**

The Word of faith is the Good News — the Gospel of Jesus Christ. When we hear the Gospel preached, we get knowledge about God, and knowledge about God also reveals knowledge about God's world — the spirit world. The Word shows us what is in the spirit realm.

> So then faith cometh by hearing, and
> hearing by the word of God.
>
> **Romans 10:17**

So then faith comes. If faith comes, then faith must come from somewhere. And faith must not have been there before it came, or it would not have had to come there. So you start out without faith, and then faith comes.

Faith does not come by praying. Faith does not come by fasting. Faith does not come by begging. Faith does not come by whining. Faith does not come by crying. Faith comes by hearing, and hearing by the Word of God. This is the way God designed the system, and you cannot change it. You cannot go around it and find another way. This is it.

Faith comes by hearing the Word of God, so the Word and faith go hand in hand. You cannot have one without the other. If you have the Word of God, then you have faith present. If you have faith present, then you have the Word of God, because the proclaiming of the Word of God causes faith to come.

I like to say it this way, "Faith and the Word of God go together like the wet with the water." You cannot have the water without the wet. You cannot have the Word of God proclaimed without faith.

Hearing Never Stops

Now it does not say that faith comes by *having heard*. This is where so many people miss it. Faith comes by hearing, and hearing is present tense — it goes on forever and never stops. You need to keep hearing and hearing and hearing. It is like eating. You have eaten in the past, but you have to keep on eating every day if you want to stay strong and healthy. The food you ate last week will not keep you functioning this week.

Minister, if you want the supernatural signs and wonders to work in your church, you cannot sit there and wait for God to do something. If you want an environment in which the Spirit of God can move, you are going to have to preach on it. You are going to have to teach on it, so that faith can come to the people who are hearing you. The environment needs to be charged with faith before the power of God can be ministered.

I used to wonder why God was not doing certain things in our church. I was waiting for God, and God was waiting for me. I did not know what was wrong. Finally the Lord got through to me that I was asking the wrong question. Instead of asking, "God, why won't You ...," I should have been asking, "God, what do You want me to do so You can ...."

Do you want healing to work in your church? You have to preach on it and then teach on it. Otherwise there will not be any faith. Faith comes by hearing. The people will not have any faith, and God cannot work. He wants to work. He wants to move among His people, but He cannot because so many churches will not let Him. They refuse to preach the Word.

So faith and the Word of God go hand in hand. You cannot have one without the other. They are so closely tied that they are almost synonymous terms. You can use them interchangeably.

This is the Frederick K.C. Price translation of Hebrews 11:1: "Now the Word of God is the substance of things hoped for; the Word of God is the proof of things not perceived by the senses."

Do you believe it, or do you just think you believe it? Do not be deceived. If you really believe it, you will say what God says instead of what the devil says.

God says Jesus **took our infirmities, and bare our sicknesses** (Matt. 8:17). *Took* and *bare* are past tense verbs. That means you do not have infirmities and sicknesses anymore. In reality you do not, but you say you do. And you will have them as long as you say you do, because then you have signed for the package, and the devil has a right to deliver it and keep it on your front porch.

This is where a lot of people go into brain lock. They say, "Now that doesn't make sense. I don't understand that. I know I'm sick. I know I've got pain. I know! Don't tell me I'm not sick."

Well, keep reading. Take a look at the other side of the coin.

> **While we look not at the things which are seen, but at the things which are not seen: for the things which are seen are temporal; but the things which are not seen are eternal.**
>
> **2 Corinthians 4:18**

In this verse, we find the words *look* and *seen*, which take us back to the eyes and the other physical senses. Two things are brought to our view: one God calls the seen things, and one God calls the not seen things. We have the seen and the unseen. Now, what is God talking about? It is the same thing He is talking about in Hebrews 11:1.

Let me paraphrase 2 Corinthians 4:18 like I did Hebrews 11:1, and you will see something that is astonishing:

"While we look not at the things which are perceived by the senses, but at the things which are not perceived by the senses; for (or because) the things which are perceived by the senses are temporal (temporary or subject to change), but the things which are not perceived by the senses are eternal."

We have to see these things by faith. And this is where a lot of people get all mixed up, and this is why there are counterfeits out there to try to draw you away from God's reality.

Beware the Counterfeits

You have never seen a counterfeit three-dollar bill, and you never will unless the United States Treasury Department decides to start printing three-dollar bills. Nobody with any sense counterfeits what does not already exist. Counterfeiters always take what is already in existence and try to make copies of it. Then you get suckered into accepting the copy for the real thing.

Satan has some copies. The copies have such names as Christian Science, Metaphysics, Spiritual Frontiers Fellowship, Unity, Dianetics, Mind Science and Mind Power. Do not be deceived. Do not confuse the Bible with these counterfeits. Bible faith takes you into the spirit realm. Satan's counterfeits take you into the soulish realm, where they operate on mind power, not God's power of the spirit.

I am not talking about things that are not really there. The verse says, **While we look not at the things which are seen**. The things which are seen must really exist. If they did not exist, there would be no need to tell you not to look at them, because you cannot see what is not there. The very fact that He says not to look at it is indicative of the fact that it does exist, but God is telling you, "Don't look at that dumb thing."

"Well, what am I supposed to do, Brother Price, ignore it?"

No, you don't say that it is not there. You just don't give it any credit for having any effect or control on your life. You don't say it is not there; you just don't give in to it. Can you see the difference?

> **(As it is written, I have made thee a father of many nations,) before him whom he believed, even God, who quickeneth the dead, and calleth those things which be not as though they were.**
>
> **Romans 4:17**

Notice this: it does *not* say God calls those things which be as though they were not. He calls those things which be not as though they were. That is a vast difference.

It is saying the same thing as 2 Corinthians 4:18:

> **While we look not at the things which are seen, but at the things which are not seen: for the things which are seen are temporal; but the things which are not seen are eternal.**

24

We do not deny that sickness and disease exist. That would be foolhardy. If we do deny their existence, then God will have to change one of His seven redemptive names. *Jehovah Rapha* means "I am the Lord who heals you."

How could God heal you of something that does not exist in you? If there were no such thing as sickness and disease, then God could not be the Lord who heals you, because there would not be anything to heal.

So sickness does exist. Pain does exist, but we need to stop giving it comfort. We need to stop owning it as ours.

Look at the Word

What do you do, then, when you are in pain? Do you deny the pain? Do you say, "I don't hurt. I don't have pain. I'm not really in pain. My back doesn't hurt"? No, you ignore it for a higher vision, a higher revelation. What do you look at? You look at the unchanging Word of the Living God.

Hebrews 6:18 says it is impossible for God to lie. If it is impossible for God to lie, then the only other alternative is that God must tell the truth. So if God says that with Jesus' stripes I was healed, then I must be healed. If I am not healed, God is a liar. And if God is a liar, the Bible is invalid and of no effect.

"Yeah, but I don't feel well."

That is your problem. You are walking by your senses instead of walking by the Word of God. You say you believe the Bible, but you do not. You believe the circumstances.

I have seen too many people come to meetings to be prayed for, then the first thing they say when they leave the prayer line is, "No, no. It didn't work. I don't feel any better." And they never will.

Now, I am talking about faith here, not the supernatural intervention of God. When the gifts of the Spirit are operating, God is initiating it, and you do not have to believe anything. But you cannot walk in those signs and wonders all your life. And a lot of people lose their healing before they get out the front door, because they do not know how to keep it by faith. We must walk by faith.

4
The Power of the Tongue

Death and life are in the power of the tongue: and they that love it shall eat the fruit thereof.

Proverbs 18:21

This verse can have a profound impact on your life. Death and life are in the power of *your* tongue. That means you can speak death to your life with your own mouth, or you can speak life to your life with your own mouth. It is up to you. Everything you have in your life right now and everything you are right now is the sum total of all you have been believing and saying with your mouth over the years.

Laws work whether you know they are working or not. You can jump off the top of a skyscraper and not know that there is any such thing as the law gravity. But as soon as your foot leaves that top ledge, you are going to come under the influence of that law. You do not have a choice over whether that law works. The law of gravity will bring you crashing to the ground in a matter of seconds. That law is working twenty-four hours a day whether you know it or not.

You need to know that there is a law of words. When you speak words that are out of agreement with the Word of the Living God, you have just cut yourself off from God. It does not mean that you are no longer His child. It does not mean that He no longer loves you. But it does mean you have broken the connection.

For example, I can be talking on the telephone to my wife. If something happens to break the connection, we are no longer communicating. My wife is still on the other end of the line, and I do not love her any less than when I could hear her voice. However, the communication has been interrupted. I am on this end, and she is on that end, but we are not making contact. We are still husband and wife, but we have been cut off.

When we are not operating in line with the Word of God, we have cut ourselves off. God is still our Father. We have not broken the relationship, just the connection. We are operating in line with tradition and feelings and circumstances.

God wants us to deny that the circumstances have any right to dictate to us where we are or what we do. They are not our Lord — Jesus is.

If you want to walk in the realm of the spirit, you will have to change your vocabulary and bring it in line with the Word of God.

Snared by My Mouth

I had to do this almost twenty years ago. I was a disaster going somewhere to happen. I was my own worst enemy, and I did not know it. I had been speaking death into my life for years and had built up a reservoir of death. I was allowing circumstances to cheat me out of the benefits I should have had under the covenant.

I was being cute and saying things like, "Well, I think I'm going to be sick. I just heard that the Hong

Kong flu is on its way around again, and I'm always one of the first to get it."

That may sound funny to you, but you probably have been doing the same thing. Death and life are both in the power of the tongue.

Look at what Jesus said:

> **For verily I say unto you, That whosoever shall say unto this mountain, Be thou removed, and be thou cast into the sea; and shall not doubt in his heart, but shall believe that those things which he saith shall come to pass; he shall have whatsoever he saith.**
>
> **Mark 11:23**

Jesus did not say "whatsover is good." He said "whatsover." If you keep talking death, that is what you are going to have. If you keep talking sickness and disease, that is what you are going to have. If you keep talking problems, that is what you are going to have, because you are going to create the reality of them with your own mouth. That is a divine law.

Notice that Jesus said you will have what you *say* not what you *believe*. You will only get it because you say it. So what you say ought to be based on what you believe, and what you believe ought to be based on what the Word says.

> **Come unto me, all ye that labour and are heavy laden, and I will give you rest.**
>
> **Take my yoke upon you, and learn of me; for I am meek and lowly in heart: and ye shall find rest unto your souls.**
>
> **For my yoke is easy, and my burden is light.**
> **Matthew 11:28-30**

Jesus said His yoke is easy and His burden is light, and He is not a liar. He is the way, the truth, and the life. (John 14:6.) He said He will give you rest, not more trials and tribulations. Jesus said it, and that settles it.

Carefree Living

The reason the Christian life has been hard for many people is because they have been carrying the burdens themselves. But you do not have to carry them. If your yoke is hard and your burden is heavy, something is wrong. You need to come into agreement with what the Word says.

Look at Peter's instruction:

> **Casting all your care upon him; for he careth for you.**
>
> **1 Peter 5:7**

If I have cast my care on Him, that means he has it. If He has it, then I do not, and if I do not, I am free. If I turn around and pick up that care again, then He does not have it any longer, and I am weighed down with a heavy burden. I have to cast my care on Him and leave it there. That is the freedom God wants us to walk in.

I know it is risky for me to say this, but it is still the truth, and the truth will set you free. Since 1970, I have not had a down day. Not one. And I do not ever intend to have any. I retired from down days almost twenty years ago.

If you want them, you can have them. There are a lot of them out there — any color, size or shape you want. You are welcome to them, but I have not been discouraged in all that time.

Now, do not misunderstand me. I have had plenty of opportunities to be discouraged and down. I have had the same opportunities as everyone else, because I live in the same world and fight the same devil. But I have learned to say, "Pass on by, troubles. I am free."

I cast all my care on Him. I cast my ministry on Him; it is His ministry, not mine. I am going to do my part and carry out my assignment, but I do not have a problem with it, because it is not my ministry. The people do not belong to me; they belong to the Lord. I am an undershepherd. If I feed the sheep and feed the lambs, then Jesus will take care of the rest.

Whining and Crying

Now some people would rather listen to the devil than to the Word of God, because they get a lot of sympathy that way. They cry and whine and get their egos patted. They say, "Poor old me, the devil has been whipping me. Poor old me, ain't it a shame?" Sympathy becomes their reward instead of the benefits of the covenant.

I have not cried in almost twenty years, but my wife can tell you that I used to be a cry baby. I was a world-class worrier. I could whine in several octaves at the same time. In fact, whenever I would see somebody, I would give them an organ recital. Have you ever heard an organ recital? "My ear hurts, my nose hurts, my eyes hurt, my lungs hurt, my chest hurts, my digestive organs hurt ...," you know, an organ recital.

But I retired from all that. I cast all my cares on Him. The Lord will not touch them if we do not cast all of them on Him.

If you do not cast the cares on Him, you will have to carry the burden. The burden is real, and it will weigh you down until you can hardly walk. Pain is real. Fear is real. Poverty and lack are real. As you carry all that mess on your back, you will be bent over, struggling down the road of life. You might even be proud about what a hard time you are having.

But I am not like the six o'clock news on television. I have good news for you. You can be free in Jesus. I do not have trials and tribulations. I have opportunites for them, but I have cast all my cares on Him, because He cares for me. If I have cast them on Him, then I do not have them, and I am free. If I say I am not, I am a liar, and I am going to have the power of Satan working in my life, because I am going contrary to what the Word of God says.

For years now, I have not been down or discouraged. No blue Mondays, red Tuesdays, orange Wednesdays, chartreuse Thursdays, black Fridays, green Saturdays or purple Sundays. Every day is a good day. I have had a thousand opportunities to be discouraged, but I have gone by all them, because I walk by faith and not by sight.

5
A Living Example

For we walk by faith, not by sight.
2 Corinthians 5:7

In this verse, God is saying that we should walk by the Word and not by the physical senses. The Word is our standard. Jesus is our example.

If that is true (and it is), how dare I say that I am scared or afraid? That would be pointing my bony finger in the face of God and calling Him a liar. He said in His Word:

For God hath not given us the spirit of fear;
but of power, and of love, and of a sound mind.
2 Timothy 1:7

So if I have fear, it did not come from God, and I do not have any business entertaining it. It is dishonoring to God.

Yes, I could be scared every minute of every day, but I retired from it because God has not given me that spirit. I do not need it, so I am not afraid of anything.

You may think that I have not faced the same things you have, but I have been exactly where you have been. I was there when the doctor walked out of the room and told me that my little eight-year-old son, who had been run over by a car, was dead. I have walked there.

I stood by the casket of my wife's younger sister who died of cancer. Then shortly thereafter, someone jumped in the car behind her husband and blew his brains out. Shortly after he was killed, their oldest son committed suicide. My wife's younger brother died of an overdose of narcotics. I have been there, but I do not talk about those things, because they do not magnify the Lord, and it is not going to bring them back to talk about it.

I stood there on the porch when they jacked up my car and repossessed it. I was there when the man with the two-wheel dolly came in the house, went over to the corner and unplugged the television set. He wrapped the cord around the back of the TV, pushed the dolly underneath it, secured the lashing strap around it, and repossessed my TV. I know what it is to have things taken away from me.

I stood in the court when I had to declare bankruptcy, because I could not pay my bills, and I could not take care of my wife and children.

Battle With Tumors

Before I learned how to walk in the Word, I had a tumor in my body. The churches that I went to then said that miracles and healing were only for the Early Church and that all that ended when the apostles died. They said it did not work anymore, but thank God for doctors and medicine.

The doctor cut that tumor out of me, but he told me another one might grow in the other side of my chest cavity later on. Sometimes vestiges of that particular type of tumor will stay in the body and travel to a new location later.

Sure enough, one day there was another tumor that grew and grew. But I knew what the Word said by that time, and I cursed the thing in the name of Jesus. It took me eleven months to stand, because I was still a baby in faith. I had more of the Word in my head than in my heart, but I kept saying, "I believe I am healed based on the Word of God."

Romans 10:17 says **faith cometh by hearing, and hearing by the word of God**. It does not say who you have to hear it from. You can hear it from your own mouth. If you cannot believe your own mouth, whose mouth are you going to believe?

If I walked up to Oral Roberts and said, "You're scared, you're scared," do you think that would bother the man of God? Of course not, because my words do not have the credibility with him that his words do. He believes his words more than he believes mine.

So when you say things like, "I'm sick. I'm poor. I can't make it. I'm afraid I won't succeed," you believe those things, because you have confidence in your words.

Crenshaw Christian Center has been out of room for more than ten years. In 1977, we went to double services. We went looking for more room and found a twenty-three acre property in Los Angeles. That was like finding pearls of great price, because there is not that much property right in the middle of the city.

Taking a Huge Loss

We went to inquire about the property, and something inside me said, "No, don't go into this deal." But we went into it anyway. It did not work out, because we did not get the financing we needed.

Finally, they gave us one last opportunity, but they wanted us to put up one hundred thousand dollars. My board said, "Yes, pastor, we need to do this. We ought to do it." Something inside said, "No, don't do it," but I did not want to be dictatorial, so I said, "Well okay, let's go with it." We lost the hundred thousand dollars. I had to stand up there that Sunday morning all by myself and take full responsibility as pastor of the church for losing one hundred thousand dollars.

A multimillionaire, white businessman called me into his big, beautiful office and asked me to sit down. This spirit-filled, tongue-talking, Bible-toting, faith-believing businessman said, "Fred, you might as well realize it. Nobody is going to loan you any money in the ghetto." That was a real encouraging word. Where were we going to get the money to solve our space problem in the ghetto?

Well, my God supplies all my needs according to His riches in glory by Christ Jesus. (Phil. 4:19.) So I began to say, "I believe that all my needs are met." We did not have any money, but by confessing the Word of God we bought a thirty-two-acre piece of property right in the heart of Los Angeles. Without selling any chicken dinners and without any rummage sales, black folks bought thirty-two acres for fourteen million dollars. We owe less than four million dollars on it now, and we are building a sanctuary that will seat more than ten thousand people.

What will we do if we cannot get it built? That is not my problem. It is not my church; it is God's church. If He cannot build it, then we do not need it. If I could build it, I would have done it more than ten years ago when we ran out of room. I cannot do it, but God can.

Perhaps you now can understand me better when I say that I do not have any problems. I have cast them all on Him. So I have to act like I am free, and I have to talk like I am free.

I am a living example that it works. I have confessed my way out of debt personally. I do not owe money to anyone, and I pay cash for everything. I am trying to give you a living example of a contemporary man of faith, not someone who lived hundreds of years ago. Thank God for Martin Luther, but I never saw Martin Luther. Thank God for Charles and John Wesley, but I never saw them either. We need to see some contemporary people who are walking by the Word of God and not by the physical senses.

6
Reaching Into the Realm of the Spirit

The sixth chapter of 2 Kings records some of the exploits of Elisha, the prophet of God. At this particular time, Israel was at war with Syria. Whenever the Syrians would go out and set an ambush, the word of knowledge would work in Elisha's life, and he would inform the king of Israel about Syria's plans. Time after time, Israel's troops avoided the ambushes.

This happened so often and so regularly that the king of Syria said, "We must have a fink in our ranks. Some spy is giving away our military secrets."

One of the soldiers said, "Oh, no, king, that is not the problem at all. There is a prophet over there in Israel, and he knows everything ... even what is going on in your bedchamber."

And the king said, "Send some spies to find out where this prophet is."

When the spies returned, they told the Syrian king that Elisha was in Dothan.

Then the king said, "Get the troops and chariots togther. We're going to go over and lay siege against this city. We're going to put a stop to this leak in our communications."

So they went over that night and surrounded the entire city.

Early in the morning, Elisha's servant went out to draw water, as was his custom, but this time his eyeballs almost fell out of their sockets. Everywhere he looked he saw Syrian troops.

He dropped his bucket and ran back to the house. "Alas, my master, what shall we do? The army of the Syrians has us surrounded! What shall we do?"

Elisha said, "Come and show me what you are talking about."

They went outside, and the servant said, "Look! Everywhere you can see there are Syrian troops waiting for us."

"Oh," said the prophet.

"Oh?" said the servant. "Man, we're about to die, and all you can say is 'Oh'?"

Elisha said, "Fear not, for those who are with us are greater than those who are with them."

"Open His Eyes"

The servant looked at the thousands of Syrian troops, then at the two of them, and then back at the troops and chariots. He thought, "The prophet has really lost it this time. He can't see, or else he can't count."

And Elisha prayed, and said, Lord, I pray thee, open his eyes, that he may see (2 Kings 6:17).

Wait a minute. What kind of nonsensical prayer is this? The prophet is saying, "Lord, open his eyes," when the servant's eyes were already wide open. That is what had scared the poor dude so much.

But the prophet was not talking about the servant's physical eyes. He was talking about the eyes of the spirit — the eyes that see beyond what the physical eyes can perceive.

So the Lord opened the spiritual eyes of the young man, **and, behold, the mountain was full of horses and chariots of fire round about Elisha** (v. 17).

Everything Elisha needed was already in the spiritual realm. Even when the servant could not see the horses and chariots of fire, they were still already there. The spirit world is more real than the physical world. The physical world is only a shadow of that real world — the realm of the Spirit of God.

Whether you see it or not, and whether you feel it or not, everything you need that is consistent with a godly life is already in the spirit realm. You have to speak it from the spirit realm into this three-dimensional physical world. If it is consistent with a godly life, you can have it.

You initiate it by your faith, and that takes effort and determination. Some people want God to pour it out on them without any effort on their part. But 2 Corinthians 5:7 says, **we walk by faith**. It does not say, "God pushes." It says, "We walk."

You *can* walk above the circumstances of life. That is walking by the Word and not by the senses. That is casting all your cares on God and taking Him at His Word. That is bringing the supernatural realm into the natural realm.

About the Author

Dr. Frederick K.C. Price is the founder and pastor of Crenshaw Christian Center in Los Angeles, California. He is known worldwide as a teacher of the biblical principles of faith, healing, prosperity and the Holy Spirit. During his more than 47 years in ministry, countless lives have been changed by his dynamic and insightful teachings that truly "tell it like it is."

His television program, *Ever Increasing Faith*, has been broadcast throughout the world for more than 20 years and airs in 15 of the 20 largest markets in America, reaching an audience of more than 15 million households each week. His radio program is heard on stations across the world, including the continent of Europe via short-wave radio. He is the author of more than 50 popular books teaching practical application of biblical principles.

Dr. Price pastors one of America's largest church congregations, with a membership of 20 thousand. The church sanctuary, the FaithDome, is among the most notable and largest in the nation, with seating capacity of more than 10 thousand.

In 1990, Dr. Price founded the Fellowship of Inner City Word of Faith Ministries (FICWFM). Members of FICWFM include more than 300 churches from all over the United States and various countries. The Fellowship, which meets regionally throughout the year and hosts an annual convention, is not a denomination. Its mission is to provide fellowship, leadership, guidance and a spiritual covering for those desiring a standard of excellence in ministry. Members share methods and experiences commonly faced by ministries in the inner cities. Their focus is how to apply the Word of Faith to solve their challenges.

Dr. Price holds an honorary Doctorate of Divinity degree from Oral Roberts University and an honorary diploma from Rhema Bible Training Center.

On September 6, 2000, Dr. Price was the first black pastor to speak at Town Hall Los Angeles. In 1998, he was the recipient of two prestigious awards: The Horatio Alger Award, which is given each year. This prestigious honor is bestowed upon ten "outstanding Americans who exemplify inspirational success, triumph over adversity, and an uncommon commitment to helping others ...." He also received the 1998 Southern Christian Leadership Conference's Kelly Miller Smith Interfaith Award. This award is given to clergy who have made the most significant contribution through religious expression affecting the nation and the world.

Books by
Frederick K.C. Price, D.D.

THE PURPOSE OF PROSPERITY

INTEGRITY
The Guarantee for Success

HIGHER FINANCE
How to Live Debt-Free

RACE, RELIGION & RACISM, VOLUME 1
A Bold Encounter With Division in the Church

RACE, RELIGION & RACISM, VOLUME 2
Perverting the Gospel to Subjugate a People

RACE, RELIGION & RACISM, VOLUME 3
Jesus, Christianity and Islam

THE TRUTH ABOUT ... THE BIBLE

THE TRUTH ABOUT ... DEATH

THE TRUTH ABOUT ... DISASTERS

THE TRUTH ABOUT ... FATE

THE TRUTH ABOUT ... FEAR

THE TRUTH ABOUT ... HOMOSEXUALITY

THE TRUTH ABOUT ... RACE

THE TRUTH ABOUT ... WORRY

THE TRUTH ABOUT ... GIVING

Living in the Realm of the Spirit

LIVING IN HOSTILE TERRITORY
A Survival Guide for the Overcoming Christian

DR. PRICE'S GOLDEN NUGGETS
A Treasury of Wisdom for Both Ministers and Laypeople

BUILDING ON A FIRM FOUNDATION

FIVE LITTLE FOXES OF FAITH

THE CHRISTIAN FAMILY:
Practical Insight for Family Living

IDENTIFIED WITH CHRIST:
A Complete Cycle From Defeat to Victory

THE CHASTENING OF THE LORD

TESTING THE SPIRITS

BEWARE! THE LIES OF SATAN

THE WAY, THE WALK,
AND THE WARFARE OF THE BELIEVER
(A Verse-by-Verse Study on the Book of Ephesians)

THREE KEYS TO POSITIVE CONFESSION

THE PROMISED LAND
(A New Era for the Body of Christ)

A NEW LAW FOR A NEW PEOPLE

THE VICTORIOUS, OVERCOMING LIFE
(A Verse-by-Verse Study on the Book of Colossians)

Books by Frederick K.C. Price, D.D.

NAME IT AND CLAIM IT!
The Power of Positive Confession

PRACTICAL SUGGESTIONS FOR
SUCCESSFUL MINISTRY

WALKING IN GOD'S WORD
Through His Promises

HOMOSEXUALITY:
State of Birth or State of Mind?

CONCERNING THOSE WHO HAVE FALLEN ASLEEP

THE ORIGIN OF SATAN

LIVING IN THE REALM OF THE SPIRIT

HOW TO BELIEVE GOD FOR A MATE

THANK GOD FOR EVERYTHING?

FAITH, FOOLISHNESS, OR PRESUMPTION?

THE HOLY SPIRIT —
The Missing Ingredient

NOW FAITH IS

HOW TO OBTAIN STRONG FAITH
Six Principles

IS HEALING FOR ALL?

HOW FAITH WORKS

FAITH'S GREATEST ENEMIES

To receive Dr. Price's book and tape catalog
or be placed on the EIF mailing list,
please call:

(800) 927-3436

*Books are also available
at local bookstores everywhere.*

For more information, please write:

**Crenshaw Christian Center
P.O. Box 90000
Los Angeles, CA 90009**

or check your local TV listing:

**Ever Increasing Faith
Television Program**

or visit our Websites:

**www.faithdome.org
www.faithdome.tv**